The Smart Investor's Guide to Alternative Investment Success

A Practical Guide to Navigating the World of Alternative Investments

Joshua Luberisse

Fortis Novum Mundum

Copyright © 2023 Fortis Novum Mundum

All rights reserved

The characters and events portrayed in this book are fictitious. Any similarity to real persons, living or dead, is coincidental and not intended by the author.

No part of this book may be reproduced, or stored in a retrieval system, or transmitted in any form or by any means, electronic, mechanical, photocopying, recording, or otherwise, without express written permission of the publisher.

CONTENTS

Title Page
Copyright
Disclaimer
Chapter One: What are Alternative Investments — 3
Chapter Two: Importance of Alternative Investments — 5
Chapter Three: Types of Alternative Investments — 8
Chapter Four: Advantages and Disadvantages of Alternative Investments — 17
PART II: Direct Participation Programs (DPPs) — 20
Chapter Five: Introduction to Direct Participation Programs — 21
Chapter Six: Advantages and Disadvantages of DIRECT PARTICIPATION PROGRAMs — 23
PART III: Real Estate Investment Trusts (REITs) — 26
Chapter Seven: Introduction to Real Estate Investment Trusts (REITs) — 27
Chapter Eight: Advantages and Disadvantages of REITs — 32
PART IV: Limited Partnerships (LPs) — 35
Chapter Nine: Introduction to Limited Partnerships — 36
Chapter Ten: Advantages and Disadvantages of LPs — 39
PART V: Conclusion — 42
Chapter Eleven: Glossary of Terminology — 43

Chapter Twelve: Recap of Key Concepts	51
About The Author	53
Books By This Author	55

DISCLAIMER

DISCLAIMER: Any content provided herein should not be relied upon as advice or construed as providing recommendations of any kind. It is your responsibility to confirm and decide which trades to make. Trade only with risk capital; that is, trade with money that, if lost, will not adversely impact your lifestyle and your ability to meet your financial obligations. Past results are no indication of future performance. In no event should the content of this correspondence be construed as an express or implied promise or guarantee.

Trading carries a high level of risk, and may not be suitable for all investors. Before deciding to invest you should carefully consider your investment objectives, level of experience, and risk appetite. The possibility exists that you could sustain a loss of some or all of your initial investment and therefore you should not invest money that you cannot afford to lose.

Futures, stocks and options trading involves substantial risk of loss and is not suitable for every investor. The valuation of futures, stocks and options may fluctuate, and, as a result, clients may lose more than their original investment. The impact of seasonal and geopolitical events is already factored into market prices. The highly leveraged nature of futures trading means that small market movements will have a great impact on your trading account and this can work against you, leading to large losses or can work for you, leading to large gains.

The author of this course is not responsible for any losses incurred as a result of using any of our trading strategies. Loss-limiting strategies such as stop loss orders may not be effective because market conditions or technological issues may make it impossible to execute such orders. Likewise, strategies using combinations of options and/or futures positions such as "spread" or "straddle" trades may be just as risky as simple long and short positions. Information provided in this correspondence is intended solely for informational purposes and is obtained from sources believed to be reliable. Information is in no way guaranteed. No guarantee of any kind is implied or possible where projections of future conditions are attempted.

None of the content published constitutes a recommendation that any particular security, portfolio of securities, transaction or investment strategy is suitable for any specific person. None of the information providers or their affiliates will advise you personally concerning the nature, potential, value or suitability of any particular security, portfolio of securities, transaction, investment strategy or other matter.

By reading this document, the reader agrees that under no circumstances is the author responsible for any losses, direct or indirect, which are incurred as a result of the use of the information contained within this document, including but not limited to errors, omissions, or inaccuracies.

The Smart Investor's Guide to Alternative Investment Success
BY
Joshua Luberisse

PART I: Introduction to Alternative Investments

Welcome to this guide on Alternative Investments. In this introductory unit, we will first explore what alternative investments are and then why they are important. We will also provide an overview of the types of alternative investments that will be covered in the book, including Direct Participation Programs (DPPs), Real Estate Investment Trusts (REITs), and Limited Partnerships.

CHAPTER ONE: WHAT ARE ALTERNATIVE INVESTMENTS

Alternative investments are a class of financial instruments that are not traditional stocks, bonds, or cash. These non-traditional assets include private equity, real estate, hedge funds, commodities, and other non-conventional assets. They are referred to as "alternative" because they are not as accessible or as well-known as conventional investments. The terms "traditional" and "alternative" should not imply that alternative investments are necessarily new or recent additions to the investment universe. Real estate and commodities, arguably two of the oldest types of investments, are examples of alternative investments.

Alternative investments typically exhibit a significant number of the following characteristics:

- The investment managers' narrow specializations in their respective fields
- Low correlation between returns and those of traditional investments.
- Investments with less regulation and less transparency than conventional ones
- Limited historical data on risk and return
- Unique legal and tax considerations
- Enhanced charges, frequently including performance

and incentive fees
- Portfolios that are heavily weighted in one asset class
- Restrictions placed on the ability to redeem (also known as "lockups" and "gates")

CHAPTER TWO: IMPORTANCE OF ALTERNATIVE INVESTMENTS

Alternative investments are an essential component of a diversified portfolio. They can provide a source of returns uncorrelated with the stock market, thereby reducing portfolio risk. In addition, alternative investments can provide access to asset classes and investment strategies that are unavailable via traditional investments.

In this chapter, we will delve deeper into the importance of alternative investments and why they should be considered as part of a diversified investment portfolio. We will explore the benefits of alternative investments, including the potential for higher returns, lower correlation to traditional stock and bond markets, and access to unique investment opportunities.

The four main benefits of Alternative Investments are:

1. Diversification benefits: One of the main benefits of alternative investments is their ability to provide diversification to a portfolio. This is because alternative investments often have returns that are not correlated to traditional stock and bond markets. For example, while the stock market may be performing poorly, real estate investments may still be generating positive returns. By investing in alternative assets, an investor can potentially reduce overall portfolio risk and increase returns.
2. Higher Potential Returns: Alternative investments may also offer the potential for higher returns than traditional investments. This is because they often involve investing in assets that are not as widely available or as well-known as traditional investments. Additionally, alternative investments may offer a higher yield than traditional investments, such as bonds.
3. Access to Unique Investment Opportunities: Alternative investments also provide access to unique investment opportunities that may not be available through traditional investments. For example, investing in a Direct Participation Program (DPP) allows an investor to own a direct interest in a specific income-producing asset such as an oil and gas well. Limited Partnerships also provide access to unique investment opportunities which are not available through traditional investments.

4. Considerations: It's important to note that alternative investments also come with their own set of risks and challenges. Some alternative investments may be illiquid, meaning it may be difficult to sell the investment quickly, and the value of the investment may be affected by factors such as market conditions and economic conditions, which may be different from traditional investments. It's also important to note that alternative investments may not be suitable for all investors.

Summary & Recap:

In this chapter, we have discussed the importance of alternative investments and how they can be used to diversify a portfolio and provide access to unique investment opportunities. However, it's important to be aware of the risks and challenges associated with these investments and to consult a financial advisor before investing. In the next chapters, we will delve deeper into the specific types of alternative investments and provide strategies for successful investing in them.

CHAPTER THREE: TYPES OF ALTERNATIVE INVESTMENTS

There are two broad categories of Alternative Investments: Tangible and Intangible:

Alternative Investments Types

```
                    Alternative Investments
                    /                    \
               Tangible                Intangible
               /  |  \                  /  |  \
       Precious  Real Estate/  Hedge   Venture  Private
       Metals    Commodity     Funds   Capital  Equity
       Collectibles                             Cryptocurrency
```

Tangible Investments
Tangible Investments are the various alternative investment types that are designed for the acquisition of assets that have a physical existence. It is considered a tangible investment when an investor spends money on real estate, personal property, or other hard assets. Some of these assets are evaluated based on their potential for appreciation, while the remainder are maintained based on their ability to generate income as they depreciate. For instance, collectibles have a high potential for appreciation, and as a result, their value is evaluated in accordance with that possibility. On the other hand, leased equipment is evaluated based on its degree of depreciation.

Intangible Investments
Investing in intangible assets involves putting money into things that cannot be touched or examined, but whose status and value can be tracked and evaluated based on how well they perform in the market. Some of the asset classes that belong to this

category include Intellectual Property Rights, Hedge Funds, Angel Investments, Private Equity,

Although there are insurmountable number of categories of alternative investments, in this book, we will focus on three of the most popular: Direct Participation Programs (DPPs), Real Estate Investment Trusts (REITs), and Limited Partnerships.

Direct Participation Programs, also known as DPPs, are investments that are made in particular assets that produce income, such as oil and gas wells, real estate, or equipment leasing. Instead of just buying shares of a company, investors can own a direct interest in the underlying assets through the use of direct participation programs (DPPs).

Real Estate Investment Trusts (REITs) are companies that own and operate income-producing real estate. They provide investors with the ability to invest in real estate without the need to own and manage property themselves.

Limited Partnerships are a type of partnership in which one partner (the general partner) is responsible for running the company and the other partners (the limited partners) provide capital and financial backing. In general, limited partners do not take part in the day-to-day management of the partnership, and their liability for the debts incurred by the partnership is limited to the amount that they have invested in the business.

Categories of Alternative Investments Not Covered in this book include:

Precious Metals
Gold and silver are popular alternatives to traditional investments. Some investors view them as a safe store of value and an effective inflation hedge. Investors can purchase precious metals directly, through exchange-traded funds (ETFs),

or through mining stocks. Even though precious metals have high levels of liquidity, they can be extremely volatile during stock market declines.

Commodities
Individuals can invest in agriculture, metal, and energy, among other natural resources. This includes coffee, sugar, beef, and corn as raw materials. Typically, investors engage in commodity trading through the use of futures contracts or ETFs.

Equity Crowdfunding
Through equity crowdfunding platforms, investors can buy a piece of startup companies. In contrast to traditional crowdfunding, investors acquire actual equity in the company. This is a risky investment because investors may lose their entire investment if the startup fails. Alternatively, if a startup is successful, investors can realize substantial returns.

Art
Historically, only high-net-worth individuals were able to invest in art; however, there are new ways to enter this market through shares and crowdfunding. Additionally, interested investors can purchase index funds that track the art market.

Wine
Because wineries only produce a limited number of bottles per year, expensive wine is an investment. As time passes, the number of bottles of each type of wine decreases, increasing the value of each bottle as long as demand remains constant. Changes in temperature and precipitation patterns may have a negative impact on growing conditions for wine, which is a metaphor for climate change.

Angel Investing and Private Equity
Through angel investing and private equity, individuals can invest in private companies. This may be accomplished independently or via a private equity firm. This is considered a high-risk investment, but it can be quite profitable if a private company goes

public or is acquired.

Collectibles

Collectible investments consist of coins, Beanie Babies, baseball cards, and comic books, among other items with limited availability. Collectibles are only as valuable as the price someone is willing to pay for them. Therefore, although a particular baseball card or vintage toy in its original packaging may technically be worth a certain amount, an investor will only earn a profit if he or she can find a buyer. Most collectibles are too common to have significant value, but they can be entertaining to possess. Even virtual collectibles can be purchased with non-fungible tokens (NFTs).

Burial Plots

People seeking an alternative to conventional real estate can profitably buy and sell cemetery burial plots. Investors in burial plots purchase plots directly from cemeteries, hold on to them, and then potentially resell them at a profit.

Hedge Funds

A hedge fund is a pooled investment fund that invests in a wide variety of assets, ranging from public companies to futures on commodities. They tend to invest in riskier assets and sometimes sell short, which is a risky bet against the success of a company. The majority of hedge funds require accredited investors, while others are open to all investors. Because they are funds of hedge funds, the funds available to non-accredited investors are referred to as funds of funds. This is a roundabout method of investing in hedge funds.

Distressed Debt

Investing in distressed debt involves purchasing a company's debt with the expectation that it will be repaid. Investing in distressed debt financial instruments is extremely risky due to the fact that the issuing companies are failing or on the verge of bankruptcy, thereby reducing the likelihood that they will be able to repay the debt. If they do, however, the returns are typically substantial. Investing in ETFs that hold very high yield fixed income securities is a comparable strategy.

Structured Notes
Structured notes are prevalent in Europe and gaining popularity in the United States. A financial institution issues a structured note with both bond and derivative components. The objective of a structured note is to pay out a specified sum based on market conditions. Essentially, it is common to sacrifice some upside in order to protect against severe declines. An investor or advisor can create a structured note by customizing the bond's maturity, selecting underlying assets, targeting a specific return, and determining the level of protection desired. Although fees have decreased in this area, they can still be costly. Additionally, the structured note is backed by the issuer's credit, so default risk exists.

Tax Liens
When property owners are unable to pay their property taxes and default on their loans, some municipal governments auction off their tax liens. This enables municipalities to collect taxes plus interest. Investors who purchase tax liens are granted the right to collect on the liens' payments. In some instances, if the property owner is unable to pay, the lienholder may acquire ownership of the foreclosed home.

Income-Based Repayment (IBR) Plans
With IBR loans, accredited investors can invest in offerings with payouts contingent on the repayment of student loan debts. In an effort to ensure a high repayment rate, sites offering these products examine schools and historical default rates.

Mineral Claims
The owners of mineral-rich properties can sell the rights to extract those minerals to mining companies. Minerals can include diamonds, coal, and petroleum. Investors can also purchase

mineral rights and convert them into a source of income.

Farmland
Similar to other types of real estate, farmland tends to appreciate over time. Landowners can also lease or sharecrop their land to generate income. Typically, this is a long-term investment.

Timberland
Typically, the value of trees increases over time, so investors can purchase timberland with the intention of earning a profit after the trees are harvested. Timberland is a tangible asset that has historically produced higher returns than stocks.

Equipment Leasing
This long-term investment enables investors to purchase shares of funds that own equipment that is leased to businesses. This may include medical supplies, construction vehicles, and other equipment.

Trade Finance
When companies ship materials and products across international borders, they must pay import and export fees. To finance these expenses, businesses obtain loans or private investment. Investors can help finance these transactions and receive interest in return.

Finance for the Marine and Aviation Industries
In order to finance the construction and acquisition of ships and aircraft, companies obtain loans or private investment. This kind of investment carries the potential for significant losses due to the fact that shifts in tariffs or the state of the global economy can have an effect on the market, but there is also the possibility of significant profits.

Film
Films are an investment that can be both fun and risky, and if they are successful, they have the potential to earn a significant amount of money; however, there are a great number of factors

that go into making them successful. Even though there are hedge funds and private equity funds that invest in films, getting involved in film investing can be very difficult if you do not have a comprehensive understanding of the industry.

Franchise
Buying a franchise is one way for investors to generate a steady income and profit from growth. Notable franchises include McDonald's, Taco Bell, and Dunkin' Donuts. Investors can purchase one or more locations, giving them an instant brand-recognition business. These franchises can generate income and also be sold for a profit. However, investing in franchises is not a passive investment and requires significant effort.

Intellectual Property Rights
Images, inventions, and names are all examples of things that fall under the umbrella of "intellectual property," or IP. IP has the potential to increase in value indefinitely, but it is difficult to choose which IP to invest in. One approach is known as brand investing, and it entails looking for the next big brand to emerge in the marketplace.

Infrastructure
Infrastructure investors frequently seek predictability and steady returns from their investments. A "brownfield" investment is one that involves funding ongoing infrastructure projects, for instance. These assets are being sold or leased by the current owner (often the government) and have historical data that an investor can analyze.
Infrastructure investments include:
- Transportation (toll roads, bridges, railways, public transit) (toll roads, bridges, railways, public transit).
- Utilities (dams, power stations, gas plants) (dams, power stations, gas plants).
- Communication, among many others (broadcasting facilities, Internet backbone).
- Some infrastructure projects are sponsored by the

government, while others are privately funded.

CHAPTER FOUR: ADVANTAGES AND DISADVANTAGES OF ALTERNATIVE INVESTMENTS

ADVANTAGES OF DIRECT ALTERNATIVE INVESTMENTS

There are numerous reasons why investors may wish to include alternative investments in their portfolios. They may offer protection from the stock market's volatility and the potential for high returns. Listed below are some advantages of alternative investments.
- Increased portfolio diversification
- Reduced stock market risk exposure
- Potential for above-average returns (for instance, the best hedge funds aim for returns between 25 and 30 percent)
- Certain alternatives can hedge against inflation and rising interest rates
- May have lower transaction costs
- Appeal to an individual's personal areas of interest, such as art or wine
- A portfolio that includes some hand-picked alternatives can make it easier to adhere to a long-term strategy, as opposed to a predetermined portfolio. This belief is based on the behavioral bias known as the endowment effect, which states that individuals place a higher value on items they own than on the same asset owned by another individual.

DISADVANTAGES OF DIRECT ALTERNATIVE INVESTMENTS

Alternative investments have disadvantages, just like any other type of investment. When researching and considering alternative investments, it is vital for investors to conduct their due diligence.

These are some disadvantages to consider:
- Can be less liquid than traditional investments due to the

limited availability of buyers and the absence of a convenient market Occasionally, investors must hold their funds in an asset for at least five years.
- May have high minimum investment requirements
- May have high upfront investment fees
- May have less available data and transparency about performance
- Often higher risk or more volatile
- Vulnerable to fraud and investment scams because they are unregulated ·
- Alternative assets may be less accessible, as they may not be available in 401(k) or traditional IRA accounts.

PART II: DIRECT PARTICIPATION PROGRAMS (DPPS)

CHAPTER FIVE: INTRODUCTION TO DIRECT PARTICIPATION PROGRAMS

Direct participation programs, also known as DPPs, are investments in enterprises that give the investor the opportunity to "directly" share in the earnings or losses of the company in which they have invested. An investment in the DPP could be related to anything from a supermarket to an oil drilling project. When a business initiative is successful, the investors receive their returns, just as they would with any other type of investment.

The corporate structure of a DPP is what sets it apart from other types of investments, and the fact that it gives investors the opportunity to feel more personally attached to their money is another distinctive feature. Investors in DPPs take part in all of the issuer's financial operations, in contrast to stockholders, who only have a limited ownership stake in the company through their traditional stock holdings. The capacity of a DPP to hand down losses to its shareholders is the fundamental characteristic of this type of investment vehicle.

Passing through losses doesn't sound great. Who would want a loss? However, when DPPs pass their losses through to their investors, they are in fact giving a tax benefit for those investors. The more tax-reportable losses an investor has, the more they are able to pay a lower effective tax rate. When a DPP incurs significant expenses or suffers a loss as a business, the loss is "passed through" to its investors, allowing those investors to claim a tax deduction as a result of the loss.

Traditional investments, such as a mutual fund, can only provide profits and income to their owners in the form of capital gains and income. Investors in DPPs are eligible to receive tax deductions for their share of the company's income, profits, and losses from their taxes. Even though they offer better tax advantages, Direct Participation Programs may not be suitable for every investor. We will need to go over the DPP structures in order to gain a better understanding of this.

CHAPTER SIX: ADVANTAGES AND DISADVANTAGES OF DIRECT PARTICIPATION PROGRAMS

ADVANTAGES OF DIRECT

PARTICIPATION PROGRAMS

ROI:
You can expect a return on investment of between 5% and 7%. Non-liquid assets can enhance your portfolio. Do market declines terrify you to the point of insanity? Because the DPP is an investment that will last for more than a decade, you can be certain that your money won't be touched in the near future, giving you peace of mind.

Alternative Investment Options:
It is essential to diversify your income and investment portfolio. Because of this, alternative investments might help you diversify your portfolio beyond the traditional stock market possibilities.

Limited investment equals restricted liability:
Investors perceive DPPS investments to be passive vehicles. Consequently, you are not legally accountable in the event of a lawsuit or if a business faces prosecution. However, the general partner or company would still face difficulties under such circumstances.

DISADVANTAGES OF DIRECT PARTICIPATION PROGRAM

Income threshold requirement:
The required minimum yearly income for participation in some programs and states is now set at $70,000, while the required minimum net worth is also set at $70,000. Others might require $250,000 net wealth. This may prevent some investors from investing in DPPs.

Limited company financial disclosures:
Because some companies are not publicly traded, you may not always have access to certain financial documents. Which implies you could be missing out on some important company information.

Long-term illiquidity:
DPPs aren't liquid investments, which means you can't touch them during their lifespan. This could range between 5 and 10 years.

PART III: REAL ESTATE INVESTMENT TRUSTS (REITS)

CHAPTER SEVEN: INTRODUCTION TO REAL ESTATE INVESTMENT TRUSTS (REITS)

Real estate investment trusts, or "REITs," are a way for individuals to invest in large-scale, income-producing real estate. A real estate investment trust (REIT) is a type of company that invests in and manages income-generating real estate or other assets. These may include office buildings, shopping malls, apartments, hotels, resorts, self-storage facilities, warehouses, as well as loans and mortgages. A REIT, unlike other real estate firms, does not develop real estate properties for resale. Instead, a REIT acquires and develops properties for its own investment portfolio.

You have three options for investing in REITs: directly through the companies, through exchange-traded funds, or through mutual funds. There are numerous variations of real estate investment trusts (REITs) available.

Real estate investment trusts have historically been one of the asset classes with the highest returns. Most investors use the FTSE NAREIT Equity REIT Index to gauge the performance of the U.S. real estate market. The index's 10-year average annual return was 8.34% as of June 2022. The index returned 9.05% over a 25-year period, compared to 7.97% for the S&P 500 and 7.42% for the Russell 2000. Real estate has traditionally provided a higher return on investment for yield-seeking investors than fixed income, the more common type of asset class utilized for this objective. Both of these should be taken into consideration when constructing a portfolio.

Retail REITs

About 24% of REIT investments are in shopping malls and standalone retail properties. This represents the largest investment of its kind in the United States. Whatever shopping center you frequent, it's likely owned by a REIT.

When considering an investment in retail real estate, one first needs to examine the retail industry itself. Is it currently financially sound, and what are its prospects for the future?

It's important to remember that retail REITs make money from the rent they charge tenants. If retailers are experiencing cash flow problems due to poor sales, it's possible they could delay or even default on those monthly payments, eventually being forced into bankruptcy.

It is then necessary to find a new tenant, which is never simple. Therefore, it's crucial that you invest in REITs with the strongest anchor tenants possible. These include grocery and home improvement stores.

After conducting an industry analysis, you should shift your focus to REITs themselves. Like any investment, it's important that they have good profits, strong balance sheets, and as little debt as possible (especially the short term kind) (especially the short term kind).

In a poor economy, retail REITs with significant cash positions will be presented with opportunities to buy good real estate at distressed prices. The best-run companies will take advantage of this.

However, there are longer-term concerns for the retail REIT sector due to the shift from mall-based shopping to online shopping. The subsector is under pressure despite the fact that space owners have continued to innovate to fill their space with offices and other non-retail oriented tenants.

2. Residential REITs

These are real estate investment trusts that own and manage multifamily apartment buildings and manufactured homes. Before investing in this type of REIT, investors should consider a number of factors.

For instance, apartment markets with low home affordability relative to the rest of the country tend to be the best.

In cities like New York and Los Angeles, the high cost of single-family homes forces more people to rent, thereby increasing the monthly rents that landlords can charge. Consequently, the largest residential REITs concentrate on large urban centers.

Within a given market, investors should search for population and employment growth. When there is a net influx of people into a city, it is typically because jobs are plentiful and the economy is expanding. A combination of a declining vacancy rate and rising rents indicates that demand is increasing.

As long as apartment supply in a given market remains low and demand continues to rise, residential REITs should continue to perform well. Typically, the most successful businesses are those with the strongest balance sheets and the most available capital.

3. Healthcare Real Estate Investment Trusts

As Americans age and healthcare costs continue to rise, healthcare REITs will be an intriguing subsector to observe. Healthcare REITs invest in the property of hospitals, medical centers, nursing homes, and retirement communities.

The success of this property is contingent upon the healthcare system. The majority of these facilities' operators depend on occupancy fees, Medicare and Medicaid reimbursements, and private pay. As long as healthcare funding remains uncertain, so will healthcare REITs.

You should search for a healthcare REIT that invests in a variety of property types and has a diverse customer base. Focus is beneficial, but so is risk diversification.

An increase in demand for healthcare services (which should occur with an aging population) is generally favorable for healthcare real estate. In addition to customer and property type diversification, investors should seek out companies with substantial healthcare experience, solid balance sheets, and abundant access to low-cost capital.

4. Office REITs

Office Real Estate Investment Trusts REITs make office building investments. They collect rent from tenants who have typically signed long-term leases. For anyone interested in investing in an office REIT, four questions arise.

- How is the economy performing, and what is the unemployment rate?
- What are the vacancy rates?
- How is the economy of the region in which the REIT invests?
- How much money is available for acquisitions?

Look for REITs that invest in economic powerhouses. It is preferable to own a collection of average buildings in Washington, D.C. than, for instance, prime office space in Detroit.

5. Mortgage REITs

About 10% of REIT investments are in mortgages as opposed to the underlying real estate.
Fannie Mae and Freddie Mac are the most popular, but not necessarily the best, investments. They are government-backed organizations that purchase mortgages on the secondary market. The fact that this type of REIT invests in mortgages rather than equity does not make it risk-free. A rise in interest rates would result in a decline in mortgage REIT book values, resulting in a decline in stock prices.

Additionally, mortgage REITs obtain a substantial portion of their capital from secured and unsecured debt offerings. If interest rates were to rise, future financing would become more expensive, thereby decreasing the value of a loan portfolio.

In a low-interest-rate environment with the possibility of rising rates, the majority of mortgage REITs trade at a discount to their per-share net asset value. The challenge is locating the best option.

CHAPTER EIGHT: ADVANTAGES AND DISADVANTAGES OF REITS

REITs enable investors to include real estate in their portfolios. Additionally, the dividend yields on some REITs may be higher than the dividend yields on some other investments.

However, there are risks, particularly with non-exchange-traded

REITs. Because they are not publicly traded, non-traded REITs are subject to unique risks:

Lack of Liquidity:
Non-traded REITs are investments that lack liquidity. They are typically difficult to sell on the open market. If you need to sell an asset quickly to generate cash, you may not be able to do so with non-traded REIT shares.

Share Value Transparency:
While the market price of a publicly traded REIT is readily available, determining the value of a non-traded REIT's shares can be challenging. Typically, non-traded REITs do not estimate their per-share value until 18 months after their offering closes. This could be years after your initial investment. Consequently, you may be unable to assess the value and volatility of your non-traded REIT investment for an extended period of time.

Distributions May Be Paid from Offering Proceeds and Borrowings:
The relatively high dividend yields of non-traded REITs compared to those of publicly traded REITs may attract investors. However, unlike publicly traded REITs, non-traded REITs frequently pay out more than their funds from operations. They may utilize offering proceeds and borrowings for this purpose. This practice, which is uncommon among publicly traded REITs, reduces the value of the shares and the cash available for the company to acquire additional assets.

Conflict of Interest:
Due to the potential for conflicts of interest, non-traded REITs typically hire a manager from the outside rather than promote from within. This may result in conflicts of interest with shareholders. For instance, the REIT may pay significant fees to the external manager based on the number of property acquisitions and assets under management. These fee incentives may not always align with shareholders' best interests.

PART IV: LIMITED PARTNERSHIPS (LPS)

CHAPTER NINE: INTRODUCTION TO LIMITED PARTNERSHIPS

Limited Partnerships, or LPs, are a type of alternative investment that provide investors with the opportunity to invest in a partnership while limiting their liability. In this chapter, we will provide an overview of limited partnerships, including how they work and their advantages and disadvantages. We will also discuss how to form a limited partnership investments and explain the different types of partnerships.

Limited partnerships are a type of partnership in which one partner, called the general partner, manages the business and the other partners, called limited partners, provide capital. Limited partners are typically not involved in the day-to-day management of the partnership and are only liable for the partnership's debts to the extent of their investment. This means that limited partners' personal assets are protected in the event of the partnership's failure.

FORMING A LIMITED PARTNERSHIP

The Uniform Limited Partnership Act, which was initially enacted in 1916 and has since been amended numerous times, governs the formation of limited partnerships in virtually all U.S. states. With the exception of Louisiana, 49 states and the District of Columbia in the United States have adopted these provisions.

Step 1

Partners must register a limited partnership in the applicable state, typically through the office of the local Secretary of State. It is essential to acquire all applicable business permits and licenses, which vary by region, state, and industry. The Small Business Administration (SBA) of the United States lists all local, state, and federal permits and licenses required to launch a business.

Step 2
Partnership Agreement

In addition to external filings, limited partnership partners must also create a partnership agreement. This is an internal document defining how the business will be run. This agreement outlines each partner's rights, responsibilities, and expectations. This document is referred to as the operating agreement and is not filed with any state or government entity.

The partnership agreement should outline two essential financial facets of the business. First, the agreement should specify the allocation of profits and losses. This includes the distribution of profits to partners. Second, the agreement should outline the procedure and expectations for when a partner wishes to sell their partnership interest. This may include a notice period or expectations regarding the right of first purchase from other partners.

TYPES OF PARTNERSHIPS

General Association (GP)

All partners share equally in the profits, managerial responsibilities, and liability for debts in a general partnership. If the partners intend to share profits and losses unequally, they should establish this in a partnership agreement to avoid future disputes.

A joint venture is typically a form of general partnership that remains in effect until the completion of a project or the expiration of a specified period. Each partner has an equal opportunity to manage the company and share in its profits and losses. In addition, they have a fiduciary duty to act in the venture's and other members' best interests.

Limited Liability Company (LLP)

Every partner in a limited liability partnership (LLP) has limited liability. Additionally, all partners can participate in management activities. In contrast to a limited partnership, where at least one general partner must have unlimited liability and limited partners cannot participate in management, this structure allows limited partners to participate in management.

LLPs are frequently used to structure professional services firms like law and accounting firms. However, partners in a limited liability partnership are not responsible for the misconduct or negligence of other partners.

CHAPTER TEN: ADVANTAGES AND DISADVANTAGES OF LPS

Limited partnerships are a type of alternative investment that offer investors the potential for high returns and access to unique investment opportunities while limiting their liability. However, it's important to be aware of the disadvantages such as lack of control and liquidity, and high fees.

ADVANTAGES OF LIMITED

PARTNERSHIPS:

Limited Liability:
Limited partners are only liable for the partnership's debts to the extent of their investment. This protects their personal assets in the event of the partnership's failure.

Potential for High Returns:
Limited partnerships often invest in private equity, real estate, and other non-traditional assets which can offer the potential for higher returns than traditional investments.

Access to Unique Investment Opportunities:
Limited partnerships provide access to unique investment opportunities, such as private equity and real estate deals, that may not be available through traditional investments.

DISADVANTAGES OF LIMITED PARTNERSHIPS:

Limited Control:
Limited partners typically have little to no control over the management of the partnership, which means they have to rely on the general partner to make decisions.

Lack of liquidity:
Limited partnerships are typically illiquid, meaning it may be difficult to sell the investment quickly.

Higher Fees:
Limited partnerships may charge higher fees than traditional investments, which can eat into returns.

PART V: CONCLUSION

CHAPTER ELEVEN: GLOSSARY OF TERMINOLOGY

A

Accredited Investor
"Accredited Investors" are individuals with a net worth of $1 million or annual income of $200,000 (or $300,000 joint income with a spouse); or entities with a net worth of $5 million. Additional criteria may also apply.

Alpha
Quantifies the excess return of a portfolio over the expected return, as determined by comparison to a benchmark or by a financial model. The greater alpha, the greater the outperformance.

B

Beta
Measure of the systematic (market-related) volatility risk of a portfolio relative to the market as a whole. The lower the beta, the lower the exposure to market risk (volatility) (volatility).

Buyout
An investment involving the acquisition of ownership equity in an existing company or division. The seller may be the company's parent, public shareholders, or private equity investor. The majority of buyouts involve substantial leverage and are referred to as leveraged buyouts (LBOs). If the company's current management participates in the buyout, the transaction is referred to as a management buyout (MBO).

C

Commodity
A commodity refers to a tangible good, rather than a financial asset. Every day, individuals consume commodities directly or indirectly, including industrial and precious metals, oil and natural gas, and agricultural products.

Correlation
Value between +1 and -1 that quantifies the linear return relationship between two assets and their movement. Combining investments with a lower correlation to one another can result in a more diversified portfolio. A correlation of 1 indicates that assets moved in the same direction as markets shifted. A correlation of -1 indicates that assets moved in the opposite direction as market conditions changed.

Credit risk
Risk of losing principal or a financial reward due to a borrower's failure to repay a loan or otherwise fulfill contractual obligations.

D

Derivatives
Contracts entered into with the intent of exchanging the value of underlying securities or physical assets. Generally, derivatives are used for operational efficiency or to control transaction costs.

F

Fund of funds
A fund that allocates to multiple funds and possibly to direct private transactions as well. One advantage of this strategy is that investors gain exposure to a variety of strategies and managers with a smaller initial investment (compared to investing in each one separately). In addition, a professional manager chooses investments, provides oversight, and determines when to buy, sell, or reallocate assets. Typically, funds of funds incur additional

expenses to compensate for this professional management.

Futures/Futures contract
A future is a standardized financial contract between two parties in which the buyer agrees to purchase an underlying asset (such as financial instruments or physical commodities) at a predetermined future date and price.

H

Hedge funds
Hedge funds are private pools of investment capital that have the flexibility to buy or sell a diverse array of assets. Rather than relying solely on economic expansion to generate returns, they seek to capitalize on market inefficiencies. The investment strategies pursued by individual hedge funds are extremely diverse and there is no "one size fits all" solution.

I

Idiosyncratic risk
Risk arising from the circumstances or characteristics of trading a particular security, as opposed to market movement or other macroeconomic factors.

Information Ratio
The ratio between the excess returns of a portfolio over those of a benchmark and the volatility of those excess returns. Information Ratio measures a portfolio manager's ability to generate excess returns, but also attempts to identify the consistency of the manager. This ratio indicates whether a manager has outperformed the benchmark by a large margin in a few months or by a small margin each month. Consequently, a higher Information Ratio corresponds to a greater risk-adjusted return (i.e., more consistency of outperformance).

Economic infrastructure projects (such as roads, bridges, and utilities) and social infrastructure are examples of infrastructure (schools, hospitals). Frequently, infrastructure companies monopolize the provision of a facility or service of a predetermined standard.

Interest rate risk
The sensitivity of a bond or mutual fund to fluctuations in interest rates, as measured by duration. In the event of an increase in interest rates, greater interest rate risk (longer duration) would result in a price decline.

L

Leverage
The use of financial instruments or borrowed funds to amplify performance. In a market with an upward or downward trend, leveraged investments on the correct side of the trend will experience magnified gains, while those on the wrong side will experience magnified losses.

The frequency with which investors can access their investment capital is referred to as liquidity. When investing in alternatives, specific funds' liquidity terms correspond to the liquidity profiles of the underlying investments. For instance, alternative investment mutual funds trade in highly liquid securities (such as stocks and bonds), are valued daily, and return capital to investors within a few days if they redeem. Due to the fact that traditional alternative fund vehicles, such as hedge funds, frequently invest in more complex and less liquid investments, they typically offer less liquidity. Typically, investors must notify the fund in advance of their intention to withdraw capital, and proceeds are disbursed at a later date. In the case of other long-term investments, such as private equity, investors commit for longer durations (e.g., 5 to 10 years or more). In general, it is expected that less liquid investments will offer a higher return to compensate for their illiquidity, a concept commonly referred to as the "illiquidity premium."

Long/Short
An investment strategy that employs leverage to purchase

securities that are anticipated to increase in value (go "long") and to sell borrowed securities that are anticipated to decrease in value ("short selling" or "shorting"). The objective of shorting is to repurchase the same securities at a later date for a lower price, thereby profiting from the price difference. Long-only investing permits profits from a positive outlook on a security, whereas long/short investing permits profits from a negative outlook as well.

M

Market neutral
An investment strategy that aims to hedge out all or the vast majority of market risk by taking offsetting long and short positions, resulting in extremely low or no market exposure.

N

Net market exposure is an indicator of a long/short fund's sensitivity to market direction and volatility. Lower net exposure ordinarily translates to less direct impact from market fluctuations as a whole.

$$\% \text{ LONG SECURITIES} - \% \text{ SHORT SECURITIES} = \% \text{ NET MARKET EXPOSURE}$$

O

Option-adjusted spread (OAS)
A metric for assessing the price differences between bonds with embedded options. Typically, a higher OAS indicates a riskier bond.

P

Private equity
The ownership of a company or a portion of a company that is not publicly owned, quoted, or traded on a stock exchange. From an investment standpoint, private equity generally refers to

equity-related finance (pools of capital formed by funds or private investors) designed to bring about a change in a private company, such as assisting in the growth of a new business, implementing operational change, taking a public company private, or financing an acquisition.

Q

Qualified Purchasers
Individuals with at least $5 million in investable assets or entities with at least $25 million in investable assets. Additional criteria may also apply.

R

Real assets
Tangible assets with intrinsic value, such as commodities, REITs, inflation-linked bonds, private real estate, and infrastructure.

Real Estate Investment Trust (REIT)
A corporation, trust, or association owned by investors that sells shares and invests in income-producing real estate.

Risk budgeting
Method for constructing a portfolio that focuses on analyzing its primary sources of risk. This method forecasts volatility and correlation between underlying assets and securities in order to project portfolio volatility. Using risk budgeting, portfolio managers allocate investments based on the desired level of risk.

Roll yield
"Rolling" a futures contract entails liquidating a position in an expiring futures contract and opening an equivalent position in a futures contract for the same commodity.

When the futures curve slopes upward, indicating that the price of the contract is expected to rise (contango), roll yield is negative (loss).

When the futures curve slopes downward, indicating that the

price of the contract is anticipated to decrease (backwardation), roll yield is positive (profit).

S

Sharpe ratio
Measurement of an investment's excess return per additional unit of risk (as measured by standard deviation) relative to a risk-free asset. The Sharpe Ratio reveals whether a portfolio's returns are the result of prudent investing or excessive risk. In other words, the Sharpe Ratio indicates the risk-adjusted return, which is calculated as:

$$S = (return\ of\ the\ portfolio\ minus\ return\ of\ the\ risk\text{-}free\ asset) / portfolio\ standard\ deviation$$

The rate at which new investment "signals" are incorporated into the price of a security. An example of a signal would be an analyst raising a company's earnings forecast. In efficient markets, this information is quickly reflected in the price of the security, resulting in rapid signal decay. In inefficient markets (such as certain emerging markets), prices tend to incorporate information more slowly.

Standard deviation
A measure of a portfolio's total volatility or risk. The standard deviation measures the extent to which a portfolio's returns have deviated from the mean over time. A lower standard deviation indicates less variance in returns and, consequently, a lower risk level.

T

Transparency
Level of disclosure and access to portfolio reporting, including underlying holdings and risk metrics (i.e., not just portfolio performance). Certain fund types, such as alternative investment mutual funds, are required to comply with specific transparency

and reporting requirements. For other types of funds, transparency is frequently optional and at the fund manager's discretion.

V

Venture Capital
provided by investors to start-up businesses with limited access to capital markets but a high growth potential. Typically, venture capital investments have a high risk profile but the potential for returns that are above average.

Volatility
Variations in an investment's performance, typically measured by standard deviation relative to the mean or benchmark. High volatility is associated with increased risk, as large swings in performance can make it more difficult to predict the long-term performance of an investment.

CHAPTER TWELVE: RECAP OF KEY CONCEPTS

I t's important to note that the alternative investment market is a complex and dynamic environment, and there is always more to learn. The key is to keep learning, stay informed, and consult with a financial advisor before making any investment decisions.

As you move forward with your trading journey, it's important to develop a solid trading plan that includes risk management strategies, and to continue to educate yourself on the markets and trading techniques.

The next step is to practice what you have learned in a simulated trading environment and gradually building up your experience and knowledge. Remember, practice and perseverance are key to becoming a successful trader.

I hope you have found this course informative and valuable, and I wish you all the best in your trading journey.

ABOUT THE AUTHOR

Josh Luberisse

Josh has dedicated his career to helping individuals and organizations achieve their goals and reach their full potential. With a background in business and finance, Josh brings a unique perspective to the topics of leadership, strategy, and personal development.

Josh is the author of several books, including "The Agile Leader: Navigating Uncertainty and Embracing Change with Confidence", "The Productivity Blueprint: Strategies for Achieving More in Less Time", "The Power of Persistence: Strategies for Overcoming Adversity and Achieving Your Goals", "Inflation 101: Understanding the Basics of Rising Prices and the Fed", "Smart Money Moves: Navigating the Complex World of Personal Finance", "From Rental to Riches: Building Wealth in the City that Never Sleeps" and "The Ultimate Guide to Futures Trading". These books have been praised for their practical advice and actionable strategies, making them must-reads for anyone looking to improve their performance and achieve success.

In addition to his prolific writing, Josh is a sought-after data analyst and financial consultant, working with businesses and organizations to improve their productivity, leadership, and investment strategies. With a wealth of experience and a passion for helping others, Josh is the go-to resource for anyone looking to take their career or business to the next level.

If you're looking for practical, actionable advice on how to achieve your goals, improve your performance, and achieve success, be sure to check out Josh's other manuscripts and join his community of readers and followers.

BOOKS BY THIS AUTHOR

The Agile Leader: Navigating Uncertainty And Embracing Change With Confidence

"The Agile Leader: Navigating Uncertainty and Embracing Change with Confidence" is an essential guide for leaders seeking to stay ahead in today's rapidly changing business environment. Written by a leading expert in agile leadership, this book offers a comprehensive examination of the principles and practices of agile leadership.

Through real-life examples and actionable steps, readers will learn how to navigate uncertainty, lead with emotional intelligence, and build high-performance teams. The book covers the importance of fostering collaboration and innovation, creating a shared vision and values, and developing a culture of continuous improvement.

Additionally, the book addresses common pitfalls and provides strategies for avoiding them, and offers practical advice on how to effectively implement agile methodologies within an organization. Written in a clear and accessible style, this book is suitable for leaders at all levels.

This book is a must-have resource for any leader looking to stay competitive in today's fast-paced business world. It provides the tools and strategies necessary to lead with confidence and achieve success in an uncertain and ever-changing environment. Order your copy today to gain a comprehensive understanding of agile leadership principles.

Demystifying Private Equity: A Comprehensive Guide For Investors, Finance Professionals And Business School Students

Discover the secrets of the private equity industry and learn how to navigate the complex world of investments with "Demystifying Private Equity: A Comprehensive Guide for Investors, Finance Professionals and Business School Students". This book is a must-read for anyone looking to understand the inner workings of private equity, from the different types of funds and strategies, to the importance of due diligence and exit strategies. It also explores the role of private equity in emerging markets and the future of the industry.

With real-life case studies and insights from industry leaders and experts, this book will give you the tools and knowledge you need to make informed investment decisions and pursue a successful career in private equity. So, whether you're an aspiring finance professional, an experienced investor, or business school students looking to expand their knowledge of private equity this book is the essential resource to better understand the world of private equity.

Made in the USA
Columbia, SC
21 February 2023